Rare Art & Cheap Wine

Written by:

Jared R. Calangi

book1

For Karissa,

You and I against the World.

I did not write this book for my leisure.

I had to write the words we refused to speak.

I studied poetry and art to speak the language
the both of us were too afraid to touch.

I wrote this for us.

for love.

INTRODUCTION

The boy before this book is now a runaway ghost.

Sent off. Torn from my skin. Gone.

A lost boy, unwanted in a world of wanting. Who chose to disguise all his pain with drugs, wine, and plucking at the heartstrings of any girl who was foolish enough to fall under his spell. I was the conductor of a heartbroken symphony.

Until, stumbling upon Karissa.

All instruments held at a silence. Curtains closed. The show finally came to an end.

Do not be mistaken, every girl I've touched with my hurt I saw absolute beauty in but this girl was a new force, one not to be reckoned with.

She was the only girl who was capable of touching the parts of me that I kept safe from any soul that walked its borders.

For the first time, she's the one that made me fall in love.

I refused to hurt this girl, to not see her smile was to not see the sun rise.

No part of me questioned it, I accepted the fall. I took a few steps back and admired the beauty of it all. I wrote this book to share our story.

The story of not only a feeling but an artistry.

Two sixteen year olds engulfed with a feeling so rare, it was art.

Enjoy the fall. // Jared R. Calangi

Love

Love is meditating in the middle of nowhere,
with eyes closed shut, breathing into darkness

and not being afraid when you open your eyes
that your heart is missing.

A Sense of Direction

I asked my heart to point to the soul meant for me,
to the soul crafted from the same unearthly fabric as myself.

My heart pointed at you.

Trembling Heart

The utter presence of your voice,
    alone,
was enough to make my heart tremble.

When We Met

we were strangers of the past.

Sitting upon a grass bed made for us,
your face half lit from the moon's touch.

The two of us spoke to one another as if we were lovers.

Tragic Art

She smiled with sad eyes and a drowning soul.

You were painfully gorgeous.

The Moment We Met

I turned sober.

The news stopped casting.
The wolves stopped howling.
The ocean stopped waving.

My heart broke into two.

Starry Lips

Glossed lips,
as a lone star.

In a dark room,
at a lone bar.

Injured

When you met me,
    you met the me with cuts and bruises,
    broken bones and incapable lungs.

But the moment you spoke to me:
    your voice mended me; bone by bone,
    your touch healed me; cut by cut and bruise by bruise.

I am able to breathe again.

Rare Poetry

She moves as a fine piece of poetry.
Her silhouette outlined with broken promises.

Her ink splattered thighs wrote out such a lovely soul.
A soul only found in the pages of worn out books.

Captivated, my heart begged to flip to the first page
and read her word by word,
cover to cover.

Little Things

I picked up every little piece of you.

The way you tilt your head while talking.

The way you get lost in a song while singing.

The way you tense up when I kiss you out of the blue.

　　I held on to every little thing about of you.

But especially, how at home you felt pressed against me.

Soul Searching

We were two souls in search
for one another.

Thank God
you found me.

Broken Masterpiece(s)

You are nothing less than a work of art. An unfinished masterpiece.
  Shattered marble dance at your feet.

I am here to pick up your pieces
  and though, I know you have the strength to do so yourself,
  allow these hands to help.

Guidance

Her hands guided my soul to a foreign land no other had brought.

Honey & Lemon Peppermint Tea

A resting soul resided in the fading sun.

You were smiling across a torn up wooden table at our favorite tea café. The scent of lemon lifting from the steam of your tea; honey dripped from your lips.

Your face painted beautifully, the sun stroked it's fine brush across your face. Hints of yellow hit the bridge of your nose perfectly.

A work of art. A moment of peace.

Reddened

My ears blushed when your lips met my cheeks.

Wishing Fountain

I'd skip pennies across broken down fountains and wish for what
   I desired most.

Nowadays you're by my side so I'm guessing each came true.

Winter

Cold winters made the tips of your breasts peek from your hoodies.
If only you knew I was a blizzard coming to consume you.

Your Name

Some words are so perfectly sculpted, they cannot be replaced.

1:02

I appreciated you with tired some eyes.

"lay your head down, love."
no, I would rather much look at you.

The Sound

The sound of your eyes was deafening but sweet.

In fact, I couldn't help myself from listening a little longer.

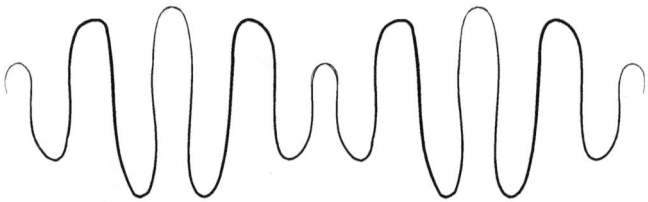

Movie Theatre

Even though you weren't, you felt like my first kiss.

The Taste of Honey

I refused to eat honey as a child. The sweet substance stuck to my hands and onto the wall of my throat, restricting me from air.

Fast forward the clock ten years, to the day we first locked lips and the memory of honey made a surprise visit.

My hands stuck to your body. I was not strong enough to let go and with my breath stolen, I fell in love with the taste of you//

//and the taste of honey.

Make-Out Sessions

My lips made you weak.
I could tell when they were dancing along your body, you dropped
to the floor with my hands guiding your back.

And each time I pulled my lips off yours, that brief second of
intimacy grabs ahold of us and we're set free.

My Clothes

I gave you my hoodies and flannels to keep you warm
   when I'm unable to do so myself.

So baby, when the world becomes a little too cold at times,
   bundle yourself up with me, entirely.

Gravity

We learned in chemistry that planets were made by gravity.
So, that explains why I gravitated towards you.

You and I are destined to build planets together.

Medicine

You were the type of medicine
with a warning label wrapped around the bottle.

Caution, do not consume with alcohol, written around your body.

Fortunately, I'm not the type of person to listen to such warnings.

November Nights

You'd be amazed with what a glass of wine and a bottle of love
is capable of doing.

A Night Out

Neon lights,
lit the night.

Cigarette in mouth,
kept my lungs tight.

Hand in hand,
all felt right.

Admiring the sky,
our star took flight.

Ecstasy

When I say you are a drug, I am not attempting to be poetic.

I mean it with the most literal sense.

Your beauty is addictive and your voice numbing.

You make the world dissipate with the slightest touch of you.

Confessions after Midnight

Didn't you like it?

How I would confess my love for you at one o'clock in the morning, with tired eyes and my chest cracked open.

Venture

Use my chest as a ship and my heart as your compass.

Allow me to love.
Let me guide you to the places you dream of.

Spring Picnic

A picnic for two,
a lovely morning
between me and you.

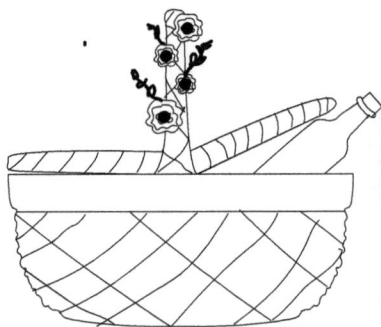

Settle

I asked your unsettling body to settle down.

I know you are stronger than the anxiety, Sweetheart.

Right

Darling, I will treat you right.

Unlike the boy from your past, an unwanted trespasser to an innocent palace, who forced himself upon your sacred body.

An action I shall never replicate.

| Between |

Cigarette between my fingers.

Smoke coming from between our lips.

My hands in between your thighs.

Our fingers meeting at the tips.

Pour

We stood in the midday sun on a cracked sidewalk with her face
buried into my chest.

My heart embraced my lover's soul, giving her a home to rest.

Her tears rolled onto my sweater. I, hugging her a little more,
a little less.

Beneath our feet, the cracks of the sidewalk began to fill with the
blood and tears of love from our chests.

For you and I, just poured our hearts to one another.

Right from Left

I am not right without you.

I am not left the same without you.

Without you, I am without myself.

Scars of Flowers

You and I laid upon a flowered bed. Snake-like vines tied our body into the ancient bed, intertwining two into one.

This bed, a garden grown for the two of us. A sunflower bloomed by your ear, a rose by mine.

Craving to know your stories, I ventured my fingers through your skin, tracing every scar. My index and middle finger stopping at your thigh. Then, once again at your spine. Making pit stops at every bump and bruise written along your body.

How'd you get this one? Where'd you get this one?

My heart beating along every syllable escaping your lips.

I now know the time when younger you jumped from your couch and the edge of your eye fought the edge of the coffee table.
&
When an eight year old you decided to carry all the groceries in your old apartment and you fell through the rickety stairs.

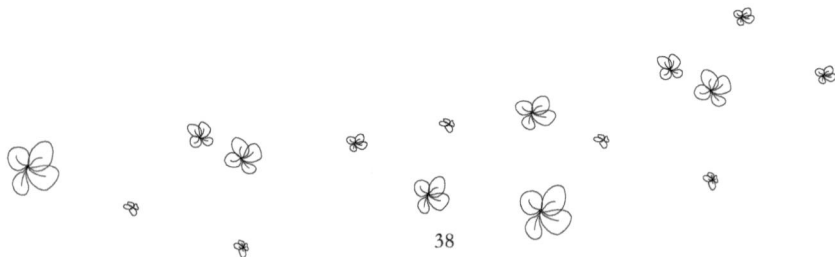

I didn't just fall in love with each scar.
I fell in love with you, deeper and deeper with each scar.

Dive into Love

I didn't just fall in love with you.

I placed my cold pale feet on the edge and dove head first.
Hands glued together, I prayed for water to catch me.

Undo

I watched you undo your bra, falling to the floor.
My heart   at your beauty, I needed nothing more.
        sunk

Ralph Lauren

Ralph wrapped around my waist,
   ripped shirt shown bare skin, for your lips to taste.

Canyons

When you would sit
the creases between
your legs and hips
sunk as canyons,
shouting out
empty echoes
of love.

Ocean

My hands reached in between her thighs and for a second,
I was brought back to the ocean.

Bruises of Love

Our hickeys were marks of a long lasting pleasure
from a love unmeasured.

"You're going to hurt me, aren't you?"

"Never."

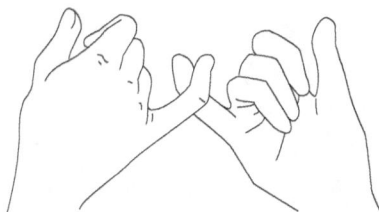

Daydreaming

Sing me a lullaby. Dream me asleep.
Once I awaken, be right next to me.

Euphoric

I touched you with gentle hands,
until your spine arched and your lips quevered.

The touch of your pleasure was euphoric.

Warm Summer Nights

We wore ripped jeans
out of all things.

Our skin stuck together
because our lips could not.

Dollar Store

Our 2 am run to the dollar store, dressed in thrifted denim
jackets and distressed jeans with a bottle of our finest love.

Hand in heart. Heart in hand.

The way the neon lights hit your face.
The way your skin looked under the cheap florescent lights.
The way I pictured you in front of the glowing ice machine.

Damn, you were beautiful.

Tied Up

I am tangled to your slender fingers.

You are wrapped under and over my aching heart.

Our souls intertwined.

I am tied to you.

Fire

She was a gentle flame and I was the fuel.

The smoke our love and nothing could possibly begin to extinguish us.

A Bottle of Love

They'd speed off at a hundred miles per hour. With no warning.
Just the nights they seem missing.

We were terrified of the bottle that drove our parents souls miles
away from their bodies.

It was in our blood. Her and I had no control over it.
The two of us still managed to stumble over our two left feet.

Her and I drunk off a feeling some may argue more dangerous.

Amour.

My Two Loves

You are the only being
that could stop me from writing.

Grip

Do not just grab my hand. Grip onto it.
Hold onto me like you'll never let go.

Hold onto me like the thought of
letting go is death within itself.

My Finger // Your Mouth

You looked so beautiful with my finger resting in your mouth.
As the wind ran through your hair and in the moment,
it felt as you and I were meant to be.

An Evening Out

Surrounded by the bodies of buildings.

The two of us fighting against the sun
and wrestling against time itself.

Making our way downtown
through the awakening lights.

It was Karissa and I against the world.

Love,

     an artistry
only you and I can touch.

Atoms

The chances of us splitting apart
is similar to splitting an atom into two.

But if the chances are against us, brace for the explosion.

It ain't gon' be pretty.

Ain't Your Average Teenage Love

We did not fall in love through computer screens.

We fell in love through midday tea dates,
and deeper through a kiss under the Christmas tree,
and deeper through the touch of our fingers,
and deeper when I wake the next morning.

and deeper...

and deeper...

and deeper...

Don't

I beg of you, love.
Please, do not break me.

You are the only thing holding me together.

Morning Medicine

I thought a glass of wine and a couple of antidepressants was
my morning medicine,

but then I met you.

Karissa Faith Pt.1,

She is rare.

A rarity placed on this Earth by the hands of God.

She is a Crystal hidden in a Sea of Rocks.

A Glowing Girl as a Glowing Star.

Karissa Faith Pt.2,

She is five feet of pure
strength,
power,
and beauty.

Do not underestimate her.

Rare Art

I pinned you against the wall and admired every part of you.

Those eyes of yours. Your lips.
The way the room vibrated from the beating of your heart.

You are what I call, Rare Art.

Found Me Dead

Two skeletons laid. Their fleshed decayed from hope and love.
Our blood dried over the years was nothing more than the thing
we craved most of.

Our tombstones were neighbored as if we were destined to be.
I dug for weeks to feel your touch and once I did, your bones
gave life to me.

Lips of Wine

Your lips held the familiar taste of cheap wine, a personal
favorite of mine.

Necklaces

She wore a golden rose around her neck,
my initials engraved onto the flower.

I wore a crystal around my neck,
specifically picked from her delicate fingers.

Our love rested at our chests for all to see.

Beat Me

You made me weaker than the others.
Your hands did more than take my breath away.

You could have beaten me to my knees and not once,
    I would have questioned you.

"I Love You."

When her lips forms those three words,
it feels like warm water running on my skin.
Touching every part of me.

Rare Art & Cheap Wine

The Toast

I cleared my throat.
Hitting the wine glass with my used fork.
The ringing bounced off the four walls.

I stood up, fixing my tie and taking in her presence.

I would like to have a toast.

I took a second to breathe in her beauty.

Cheers, to my love...
to our love,
such a rare thing.

She began to applaud for me.

Making the room feel full,
though, it was only the two of us.

Smile more, it looks beautiful on you.

Puddle

She stained my sheets,
marking where we just made love.

Summer Break

I pulled you out of the summer water. The setting sun dancing over the pool water, painting mesmerizing portraits of a love long gone.

You grabbed my white t from the leaf painted ground and began rubbing it against your drenched skull in attempt of trying to stop the water dripping from the ends of your curls.

We sat, skin to skin, with our feet sunken in the warm water.
I puffed on a half smoked joint while your hair curled up.

A love like this is not for the feint hearted.

Summer Scent

Warm summers spent
becoming drunk off your unforgiving scent.

A Taste

Our legs intertwined much like the roots of trees in love.
   I felt her warmth radiating as the morning sun does.

She reached in between shaking legs after I was done pleasuring
her soul, coating some honey around her finger for me to taste.

Magic

Wine.
Faudet.
Northern Lights.
Homemade Pasta.
Shooting Stars.
Poetry.
Art.

You.

Dreams of a Nightmare

I'm terrified of you.

Haunted house.
Bastard clowns.
Abandoned towns.

And I'm only terrified of you.

Sad Eyes

and when I realized the sadness in your eyes,
my God, my heart held on for dear life.

Parts of Me

There are parts of me that lay hidden.

Then there are parts, you yet to touch.

Father-In-Law

"Love, I think my dad would have loved you."

Breaking Her

She tried her best to fix me.
  Piece by piece.
Until it was herself falling

       a

       p

       a

       r

       t

       .

The Silent Ritual

In the moments of madness, where our clothes are being ripped from our bodies. When all worldly things become nothing but air and our hearts surrender as instruments to that one song.

There's a silent ritual, where we breathe each other in,
and our souls just be.

12:00 am

I found myself walking, a lonely ghost searching for a place to rest.

Sleepwalking to the empty swingset in the park next to her home.

I sat under the only working park light, slowly swinging, patiently
waiting for my love to arrive.

2:00 am

We snuck our feet into the jacuzzi of a neighborhood pool.

It was the middle of December, the cold Vegas air held at a still. Unmoved, no motion in our atmosphere. Wisps of steam rose from the water like ghosts from our favorite television show.

The air bitter cold, biting at our skin. I shot a glance at her, noticing nipples poking from a silk t shirt. Our thrifted jeans cuffed halfway up our calves with warm water wrapped around our ankles. The smoke of an almost dying joint warmed my lungs and reddened my eyes.

I took a final hit then flicked away the roach of the joint into the sea of ghosts. Coughing, I choked down the last drops of wine.

I reached over, collecting strands of brown hair that masqueraded her face and gently placed them behind her ear. Before she knew it, my lips were massaging her neck.

A silent moan filled the air.

The wine hit like a bag of rose petals. A drunken me pulled away from making love to her collarbone and sloppily stood up, my feet closely tripping over one another. My world spun uncontrollably but I managed to catch my balance.

"Calangi, what do you think you're doing?"

A rare grin flashed from my face but disappeared as fast as it came.

"Wanna see how it felt to fall in love with you?"

"Ha!" She flashed back a smile. "Go for it."

My wet feet took a few steps back. The pitter patter along the concrete abruptly shocked the winter air. I turned back to my love and mouthed the words, *watch this*.

Her eyes. They were watching me. Studying me. Impatiently.

I took a deep breath and sprinted toward the main pool, front flipping into the ice cold water, diving in as if it was another warm summer's day.

I felt numb. My knees buckled. My breath stolen. The water engulfed me, surrounding every inch of my skin, abusing me with pins and needles. My hair stood on end. I kicked my way back to the surface in desperate need of oxygen.

The moment my head broke the surface of the water, I gasped for life. My eyes searching to find the silhouette of my lover.

"Now, it's your turn." I said, smiling.

"Did the water give you brain damage? It's freezing, b."

I shook my head, water flying all directions. "Hurry in before my balls freeze off."

She chuckled. My lame attempt at a joke seemed enough, her feet dripping from the water of the jacuzzi and before I knew it, she was flying through the air. Her frail body plunged through the surface a couple feet away from where I waited.

I swam to her, wiping away the water that landed onto my face.

Her bone chilled hands reached up and grabbed onto my white t. She used her remaining strength to pull herself up from the heavy water.

With her legs wrapped around me, her frozen body twitched and gripped against mine.

"You're so dramatic." She teased me.

I smiled, pressing my purple lips against hers. "You know me."

Who knew two freezing lips could create fireworks?

Infinity

Endless stars to discover.
Countless days to fall for one another.

By Your Side

By your side rested me,
a joint burning between my teeth.

By your side were hidden lies,
empty bottles and lonely cries.

By your side my heart in hand,
an unseen love found unseen love.

Shadow Art

The candle that rested at the side of my bed
  illuminated our bodies.

Painting two shadows, into one.

A Lover's Body

We laid hidden,
tucked away in a foreign bed.

But somehow n' someway,
I felt at home.

At peace.

Our Hurt

We faced problems bigger than us. Problems larger than life.

A Bloody Mess

I probably shouldn't have poured my heart all over your bed sheets.

Sorry for the mess.

Fools

Our not so sober bodies laid in our unmade bed.

Her head resting on my chest and her slender fingers traced imaginary hearts onto the cotton of my white t. My hands took turns between scratching her back and massaging her ass.

Sun rays caught wisps of smoke. Her face glowing from the morning light that escaped through our lazy, lace curtains. Ashes from joints smoked the night before neighbor a half drunken bottle of cheap wine that sat at my bed side table.

The morning air felt odd. A good odd though, like the first time her and I started dating, kind of odd.

I reached into the cluttered drawer, grabbing a pre-rolled joint and placed it between my pinkish lips.

"Breakfast." I smiled, flicking to create a spark. I lit the end of Vegas' finest cannabis with my favored white lighter. Inhaling a deep hit, I filled my lungs.

She brought her still half-asleep body on top of mine. Her red laced panties meeting my Ralph.

"Jared?" She whispered into the morning air.

I grabbed her waist, pulling her body closer to mine and blew the whitish smoke towards her. Filling the air with the scent of Blue Dream. She had my full attention.

"Remember? A couple years ago, the first time we met," she paused, "I said that only fools fall in love."

I nodded my head while taking another hit.

"Somehow, someway..." pausing once again, she stole the half smoked joint from my swollen lips and placed it in between hers without taking a hit, "lil' ol' me became a fool somewhere along this journey."

Chuckling, with reddened eyes half closed. I smiled. I took the wine bottle by the neck and choked down the remaining potion. I became drunk off her eyes.

I confessed, pressing my lips softly against my lover's hand.

"I love you too, fool."

The rest of the day wrote stories only her and I should know.

Constellation of Love

Dying stars suspended above held our story of love.

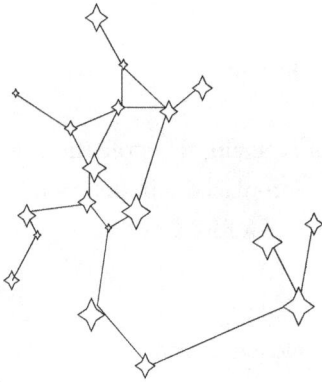

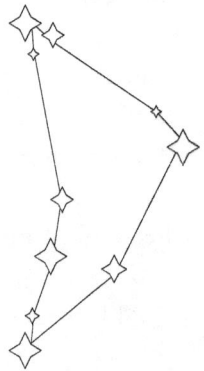

"My love, you broke me."

Crying Eyes

You are the red in my eyes
from troubled tears that yet to dry.

Our souls sloppily intertwined,
you were the soul I once called mine.

Ruined Art

I felt ruined.

Much like a painting
with it's paint smeared across its canvas.

For once, I felt human.

Pink

Pink skies cover our small town.

Pink clouds cover all around.

Pink flowers planted in soft ground.

Pink skin lost, unable to be found.

Thorny Rose

She left bloody scars at the tips of my fingers
from the struggle of picking her from the garden.

Search for Me

As much as it hurts to know you are finally moving on,
I am happy for you and the life you're building without me,
but my heart is hoping when another lover comes along,
you look into their eyes and search for me.

Slit Wrists

I would cut at my wrists,
in hope these hands fell off.

I was tired of holding these feelings for you.

Poetry Personified

She was poetry personified.

Quick to read, but most easily to leave a mark.

I could never forget your words,
even if I tried.

Butterfly Trap

Loving you?

Felt like a butterfly,
trying to escape through a closed
glass box in sight of the garden it was birthed in.

Deprived

Without your breath,
I am deprived of life.

Torn   Apart

Amputate my hands from your hips.

Destitch my lips from yours.

I dare you, go ahead.

Tear us apart.

.

Gone

Grabbing onto my bed sheets,
you whispered sweet nothings into my ear,
and before I could open my mouth to reply...

you were gone.

Day n' Night

There were days we held hands and nights we held fists
but all the while I loved you the same.

You weren't the same off the drugs...

Not Your Dream

I'm sorry I can't sing.

I'm sorry I can't dance.

I'm sorry I can't be the guy your dreams were made of.

I am Me.

I'm sorry but I'm only a writer.

Rainy Days

We laid upon white sheets.
On days where rain poured.

Now I lay alone,
    with your scent stained onto my sheets
    and your lipstick forgotten off my cheeks.

Reopening Wounds

My knuckles bled at the sight of you.

Taste of Lemon

Your lips embraced mine, without a word, whispering bitter lies.

Abandoning the sour taste of lemon on the walls of my mouth,
leaving me tongue tied.

Ms. Two Faced

Even though you were two faced,
I fell in love with both sides of you.

The Stories

I will forever remember every scar written on your body.

Always

I always search for love in all the wrong places.
I always come back to - - - - - - - - - - - - - you.

Wind

We drifted away on the same boat.

Naive Teens

Was it naive of us to fall this hard in love
this early in our lives?

4.19

"Tonight was left empty.
I was too empty to even write.

I was missing you a bit too much, my love."

The Haunting

A ghost of your past,
for I shall haunt your happiness.

Inhale

I smoke to fill my lungs from your missing breath.

Prayers

You were the lesson I had to learn.

The road that remains unturned.

The raging fire that left me burnt.

You beat me to my knees and left me begging for your return.

Problems

Loving myself was not the problem.

Loving you more, was.

Who Am I?

You spoke to me as if you were talking to
an old friend rather than an ex lover.

Heaven

Is there a Heaven for the Brokenhearted?

Night

Nights we were too alive to fall asleep in each other's arms.

Nights where we had stolen yet another bottle of wine.

Nights we got so high off each other that we didn't know what to do with ourselves.

Those are the nights I miss most,
$\qquad\qquad\qquad$ the nights that felt like dreams.

Puzzle Pieces

I did more than just love you.

Every time you touched me,
you took a piece of me with you.

And even though it hurt, I let you.

KILL ME

SO NEXT TIME YOU SLIDE THAT BLADE INCHES FROM
MY SPINE,

aim for my heart and rid me from this agony.

This is my last call,
my last hurrah.

I no longer have the energy
to fight this war,
but I shall go down swinging.

Please love,
find within
your heart,
Myself.

Please,
find me.

Search for me.

I am reaching as far as I can.

It was truly an honor to be loved by you.

Our First (Dream) Home

Steaming coffee rested on a cracked coaster.

The summer sun peeking from the horizon. *the1975's, Undo*, spun on our home record player.

  "Morning, love."

Karissa came out, curly black hair painting a perfect picture of her. Wearing only my white t, she wrapped her waking arms around my neck from behind and pressed her cherry lips against my messy bed head.

"Where'd your pants go?" I joked while she was making her way round.

"You took them off me last night," she said, sitting beside me with her legs over mine, "along with other things..." she joked.

I smiled, shaking my head. I handed her her morning tea, peppermint with a touch of honey and lemon. Karissa's favorite.

She clinked her glass, hitting my mug.

  A toast.

Waves calmy awakened the shore. Seagulls flying in search of their breakfast. Hermit crabs yawning from their shells.

We sat as one. Admiring the view from the comfort of our first home. Our warmth blanketed the two of us. With her head buried into her chest, she carefully listened to the soundtrack of my heart.

Thump, thump, thump...

Let...

Let the piano play.
Let the roses grow.
Let the snow fall.
Let the exes go.
Let the readers read.
Let the poets write.
Let the happy laugh.
Let the angry fight.
Let the smoke burn.
Let the drunk drink.
Let the ocean wave.
Let the brain think.
Let the sun set.
Let the moon rise.
Let the tired sleep.
Let the hurt cry.

Let the music loud.
Let the legs spread.
Let the shoes worn.
Let the knuckles bled.
Let the lips smile.
Let the hair curl.
Let the world turn.
Let the ballerina twirl.
Let the past pass.
Let the ghost haunt.
Let the needy need.
Let the wanters want.
Let the mind wonder.
Let the stars above.

And for god's sake...

Let the heart, love.

To the Family:

Letter I've Never Sent.

???

Try living in a house where *family* was a broken down word
no one tried to fix.

!!!

Fix it.

Please,

A Letter to my Step Dad

Dear Dad,

I hope you find this book on a shelf of a bookstore in the Philippines and pray that it brings a smile to your face with proudness in your heart.

Thank you for making me to the young man I am today. I will cherish the memories and lessons you have gifted me during the time you were here.

There is not a day that passes by that I don't miss you.

The bruises have healed and the tears have dried. You made me into a tougher boy.

Hope to see you soon dad, and though we do not share the same blood, you are family as much as anyone. Thanks for being my father when I needed it the most. Love you.

Hope you're doing well,

Your Step-Son

I'm bleeding.

A Letter to my Mother

Dear Mama,

Thank you for sticking by my side at the early age of eighteen.

I will be forever grateful for the love you poured into me, filling me to the brim and spilling more love into my younger sisters. We all realize how difficult that was.

I idolized you. Your strength. Your work ethic. You are a superhero as much as you are a mother.

I do not blame you for disappearing the past few years.

I see you trying every day. Day in and night out.

I am proud of you and I hope you are proud of me.

Love,

Your Son

Drunk

Mother, you came home a shell of yourself.

Your soul, drowning in alcohol.

You were unrecognizable.

And even though your eyes told me I was a mistake.

I forgive you.

Speak... Please

Awkward silence was the conversations my mother and I held most.

Hi, Mom

I would be quite surprised if you made it this far in.
Hope you're enjoying it. Love you.

A Letter I Never Sent to my Father

Dear Paulo Calangi,

You haven't called in a while. I don't blame you because the last time my phone vibrated in my pocket and it read your name across the broken screen, I didn't answer. I couldn't. I couldn't bring myself to press that begging green button.

I was too scared to hear your voice. A voice deepened from the pain of your past that hold across your neck.

But despite everything...

Despite the cracks of abandonment I had to grow through.

Despite all the pain you cause throughout my sixteen years on this planet.

Despite all the broken promises turned to broken bottles.

Despite all the negative thoughts that bloomed in the dark watered by the cheap wine I drank.

I (somewhat) forgive you,

- Jared Calangi

Thanks, Dad

I had to teach myself how to shave the
crappy facial hair you passed down to me.

Each time I picked up that razor the
poison of abandonment crept its way
onto the surface of my skin.

The toxin seeped into my veins,
maneuvering its way through the
trafficked streets to my heart,
eventually, killing me softly.

If I Had a Dad

Thanks for the, "I'll tuck you in's."
Thanks for helping me learn how to tie my shoes.
Thanks for being ready with a bandage when I'd get hurt.
Thanks for the unforgettable birthday parties.
Thanks for cheering me on at every sport I attempted.
Thanks for the after school ice cream.

Thanks for the annoying curfew.
Thanks for paying for my prom shoes.
Thanks for the relationship advice.
Thanks for finding my first car.
Thanks for cheering me on at my first job at the library.
Thanks for the high school graduation dinner.

Thank you for raising me. You did a hell of a job, Dad.

Aunts & Uncles

Marriage. Divorce | Death. Rebirth

Parents

The both of you hurt me more than any girl has.

You two were my first loves.
The first caring hands to touch me warm.

How could you hurt me like this?

Parentless

I grew up without a father nor a mother,
something I'd never wish on another.

Good-Bye Love

Wine held in hand, a joint resting in the other.
A drunken me, weaken from the lost of my lover.

I no longer crave the taste of honey,

of you.

Find You

I may no longer see you and I may no longer get to feel you.

But the days I miss you most,
I flip through the pages of this book and find you.

AA

I've been hungover on the thought of you.

I've been craving for a sip of your lips.

I've been imagining uncorking your top
and getting tipsy off your thoughts.

I'm just an alcoholic trying to get his fix.

Airport

Sat there listening to airplanes take flight.

I couldn't help but call you in the dead of night.

I prayed and hoped you'd answer your phone,
I had things to tell you like how I'm all alone.

Sat there in that empty airport, with no answer...
no answer in sight, just airplanes taking flight.

Airplane

Ever get so high you fly around Earth twice?

Home

You were my safe place. My sanctuary. My peace. My home.

But, all you did was leave scars on the edges of my Heart.

Painfully Beautiful

"Beauty is Pain & Pain is Beautiful."

Passion Hurts

Stop. Writing.
  You can't do this.
Please. Stop.
  Before it ends up.
Killing. You.

Colors of Hope

Purple lines circle my eyes.

Red throughout the sky.

Green clouds lazily soar.

Blue grass, grow some more.

High School

School does not define you.

School is a distraction.

A race forced to run.

P.S.

Don't stress yourself, love.
I promise you,
you are destined to do great things.
I've never been so confident.

Hide n' Seek

Do not just hear the music.

Feel the notes vibrate underneath your skin.

Tearing you apart while playing hide n' seek with your heart.

Scarlet.

Drugs You Should...

"Try it."

She urged me wearing the same exact smile I fell in love with.

. . .

And in the moments shortly after, the drug and her took control.

"You are not the man I fell in love with.
You've changed."

For I Apologize

I'm sorry for all I've done.

All clothes undone and songs left unsung.
I'm sorry for the man I've become.

"I Loved You."

There's a certain difficulty with
loving someone who does not want to be loved.

Sacrafices

Don't believe it's love,
until you're willing to let go.

Knots

Cut the ties,
they're things worth the sacrifice.

Swallow Your Tongue

When I was younger, I was taught to swallow my tongue.
   To not speak my peace.

Maybe that's why I'm such a good kisser.

50/50

As a young man,
I'm proud of my feminine qualities that were planted by the hands
of my mother, aunts, cousins, and female others.

I'm proud to be raised one part man, one part woman.

Don't Be Mistaken

Through these hands write poems of love and lost.
Though these hands plant the seeds of roses.

They're still capable of whooping your ass.

Pray 4 Love

Fight for love,
for love is tough.

Strength of love,
for my heart is crushed.

Pray for love,
for my heart was pushed.

Pushed over the edge,

falling...

                              falling...

with
no
end

.

The Absence of Presence

Bloody knuckles,
broken and bruised.

The result of the absence
of presence from you.

Why I Write?

It's beautiful.

Fight Back

The world's cruel.
People, are cruel. You know that.

You're gonna get beat up, fucked up, heartbroken.

Wear your scars.

Batter Up

All life does is throw you curveballs aimed at your heart.

Brace for it.

It's a Woman's World

I am a young man in a world of women.

Not the other way around.

Starry Night

My Love, you're beautiful.
I find your eyes when the moon is full.

Through Burning Bush

Anger rushed through burning bush,
bloody lips cut from sharpened hooks.

Self doubt flooded from judging looks,
reddened eyes hidden behind helping books.

I wish for a different self.

Water & Sunshine

Be proud of the flowers that grow on your heart.
   Take care of them.

Words of Advice

The places where you feel unwelcomed
are the places you should feel most at home.

A Lively Death

I looked through myself.
A living ghost.

A Deadly Life

Haunted by your touch.
Roaming around this land to find another to replace you.
But no other is enough.

Freedom

You cannot be free if you still allow them
to reside in your soul and occupy your heart.

Change

Embrace the change,
welcome it with open arms.

Our End

Despite the ripped jeans, we never felt close.

Never close enough to touch hips and lock lips.
But, close enough to touch the edges of my heart.

. . .

Thanks for the scars.
I'm sorry for yours.

Our Garden

We left flowers blooming in wine bottles.

I wonder how they're doing.

Relapse

After three years,
I found myself revisiting old habits.

Knocking at it's door with a gentle hello.

Head in book. Joint in mouth. Wine in glass.

I found myself again.

www.ingramcontent.com/pod-product-compliance
Lightning Source LLC
LaVergne TN
LVHW041216080426
835508LV00011B/971